While We've Still Got Feet

Works by David Budbill

BOOKS OF POEMS

While We've Still Got Feet (Copper Canyon Press, 2005)

Moment to Moment: Poems of a Mountain Recluse (Copper Canyon Press, 1999)

Judevine: The Complete Poems (Chelsea Green, 1991, 1999)

Why I Came to Judevine (White Pine Press, 1987)

From Down to the Village (The Ark, 1981)

The Chain Saw Dance (Crow's Mark Press, 1977; Countryman Press, 1983)

Barking Dog (Barking Dog Press, 1968)

COMPACT DISCS

Songs for a Suffering World: A Prayer for Peace, a Protest Against War,
with bassist William Parker and drummer Hamid Drake
(Boxholder Records, 2003)

Zen Mountains—Zen Streets: A Duet for Poet and Improvised Bass,
with bassist William Parker (Boxholder Records, 1999)

PLAYS

Two for Christmas (1997)

Little Acts of Kindness: A Poem for Fourteen Voices and Blues Band (1993)

Thingy World! (1991)

Judevine: The Play (*New American Plays 2,* Heinemann, 1990)

Pulp Cutters' Nativity (Countryman Press, 1981)

Knucklehead Rides Again (1966)

Mannequins' Demise (1965)

OPERA LIBRETTOS

A Fleeting Animal: An Opera from Judevine, with composer Erik Nielsen (2000)

CYBERZINES

The Judevine Mountain Emailite:
An On-line and On-going Journal of Politics and Opinion

SHORT STORIES

Snowshoe Trek to Otter River (The Dial Press, 1976; Onion River Press, 2005)

NOVELS

The Bones on Black Spruce Mountain
(The Dial Press, 1978; Onion River Press, 2004)

CHILDREN'S BOOKS

Christmas Tree Farm (Macmillan, 1974)

EDITED VOLUMES

Danvis Tales: Selected Stories by Rowland E. Robinson
(University Press of New England, 1995)

For more information about all of these works, go to
David Budbill's Web site at http://www.davidbudbill.com

While We've Still Got Feet

NEW POEMS

David Budbill

COPPER CANYON PRESS

ACKNOWLEDGMENTS

Some of these poems have appeared in the following magazines: *Connecticut River Review, Entelechy International: A Journal of Contemporary Ideas, Heartstone, Hunger Mountain, Inquiring Mind, Maine Times, poetryfish, The Sun, Toward Freedom;* and in the anthologies *Cry Out: Poets Protest the War* (George Braziller, 2003), *America Zen: A Gathering of Poets* (Bottom Dog Press, 2004), and *Poetry for Peacemakers* (Pax Christi USA, 2004). Grateful acknowledgment is made to the editors.

At the back of the book are a locator for the various poets and sources made reference to in the text and a findings list for translations of Han Shan poems quoted in the text.

Cover art: Gama Sennin (Chinese Hou Xiansheng) and his three-legged toad. Soga Shōhaku, 1730–1781. Japanese, Edo period (1603–1867), eighteenth century. Hanging scroll; ink on paper. Overall: 200.8 × 55.2 cm (79⅟₁₆ × 21¼ in). Image: 109.3 × 42.5, Jiku: 60.0. Origin: Japan. Freer Gallery of Art, Smithsonian Institution, Washington, D.C.: Gift of Charles Lang Freer. F1904.192

Copper Canyon Press is in residence at Fort Worden State Park in Port Townsend, Washington, under the auspices of Centrum Foundation. Centrum is a gathering place for artists and creative thinkers from around the world, students of all ages and backgrounds, and audiences seeking extraordinary cultural enrichment.

LIBRARY OF CONGRESS CATALOGING-IN-PUBLICATION DATA
Budbill, David.
While we've still got feet: new poems / by David Budbill.
p. cm.
Includes bibliographical references.
ISBN 1-55659-223-x (pbk.: alk. paper)
1. Political poetry, American. 2. Loneliness—Poetry.
3. Vermont—Poetry. 4. Aging—Poetry. I. Title.
PS3552.U346W48 2005
811'.54—DC22
2004029165

2 4 6 8 9 7 5 3

FIRST PRINTING

COPPER CANYON PRESS
Post Office Box 271
Port Townsend, Washington 98368
www.coppercanyonpress.org

Not a misanthrope, or taciturn, but friendly
and talkative rather; liking best to live alone, but fond of
tramping across the woods to gossip with neighbors.

NESSMUK
Woodcraft

Gleaning some words from old masters
I make my own poems.

RYŌKAN

Poetry is not about language.
It's about something.

JOEL OPPENHEIMER

Who says my poems are poems?
My poems are not poems.
Once you know my poems are not poems
Then we can talk poetry.

RYŌKAN

Contents

Part One

Part Two

Part Three

Part Four

Part Five

Part Seven

While We've Still Got Feet

Part One

Gama Sennin

Gut hangin' out.
Stick on shoulder.
Toad up on me
head.

Singin' me songs
on Red Dust Road,
headed toward
dead.

Thirty-five Years

Thirty-five years ago I came into this place to live
a simple life, to try to find out who I am.

Thirty-five years in these remote and lonesome hills.
Just mountains, trees, and sky, a poor farm here and there.

Thirty-five years of watching seasons come and go.
Thirty-five years gone by. Thirty-five years closer to oblivion.

Drink a Cup of Loneliness

Looking for a place to hide?
Judevine Mountain will keep

you safe. Here's the place to
lose yourself and forget about

the world. Just wind through
pines and the sound of rain.

The longer you stay, the more
withdrawn you get, the better

you'll like it here. Drink a cup
of loneliness, and see what I

mean. There's a gray-haired
guy up there who spends his

days playing flutes and writing
poems. He can tell you more.

Thirty-five Miles to a Traffic Light

From here it's five miles to the blacktop,
thirty-five in any direction of the compass
to a traffic light. People say it's way out there.

I say, yes sirree. Far out, man, say I. Far out
is what it is. Just snow and cold and isolation
and nobody to see for days and days. People get

scared by so much emptiness. So much silence
is frightening. Better not come here if you
don't want to fall in upon yourself. Better yet,

better not come here at all.

In the Tradition

For thousands of years, this urge to go away
into the quiet, to sit down and listen for that
still small voice whispering from within.

In the fourth century C.E. T'ao Yüan-ming said,
I built my hut among mankind but hear
no sound of cart or horse.

Four hundred years later Han Shan,
for the same reason, said, *The Cold Mountain road*
is strange, no tracks of cart or horse.

Seven hundred years after that, Han Shan Te-ch'ing
again built *a tiny hut perfectly secluded beyond the sound*
of cart or horse or sign of human tracks.

Another five hundred years later and here I am
on Judevine Mountain, still hoping to hear
that still small voice and saying,

Down in the valley big trucks shift down and whine
through the village. But up here on the mountain only
birdsong, rain, and wind through pines.

Up Here

The people up here,
scattered through these hills,
leave one another alone.

Their houses are few and far between.
There's nothing to do.
Cars almost never go by.

I cut wood and garden, listen for a poem.
And in the evening the house offers
books and time for music.

Directions

Sometimes people ask me how to get
    to Judevine Mountain.

I can tell you how to get to where
    the road ends, but when

you get to there, you've only just begun.
    After that I can't be

any help at all. It takes years to find
    the way. And anyhow you

don't need me. I'm lost most of the time
    myself. Besides,

how would I know what direction
    you are headed in?

Irrelevant and Useless

This place is so remote people call it Nowhere.
Hardly anyone ever comes by—except the clouds.

They visit almost every day. My only neighbors
are the birds, and they don't care what I do.

I play my flutes, read books of poems, work
in my garden, and watch the days go by.

Wealth and power mean nothing here.
This is truly an irrelevant and useless life.

Weather Report

The weather is horrible here on Judevine Mountain.
It's dark and cold all winter. Every day rain and snow

beat on your head. And the sun never shines. Then
it's spring and more rain and ice and mud, too. And

after that, the blackflies eat you alive and then the
deerflies and then the mosquitoes and then it's fall

before you ever noticed it was summer. Then there
might be a couple of weeks of decent weather and

then it starts to rain and snow again. It's just awful
living here. I don't think you'd like it here at all.

You better go find your own miserable place to live.

Part Two

Smoke and Ash

I spend every fall out in the woods, felling trees, cutting their trunks
and branches into blocks, splitting and stacking the blocks in neat rows.
I cover the wood with old metal roofing and let it sit for a year or so.
Then back to the woods with a tractor and wagon. Load the wood
into the wagon, haul it back to the woodshed, toss it in and stack it again.

All through the fall, winter, and spring I carry the wood by the armload
into the house, and stack it again in the woodbox next to the big, old
Round Oak stove. In it goes, fire after fire, day after day, month after
month. All the while I shovel the ashes into a galvanized coal scuttle,
haul them out to the garden, and scatter them over the snow.

After all that work!
A bucket of ash
and smoke
gone
into the air.

Inward

Inward to that
wilderness
pathless wood
opening
reaching out
into infinity
boundless
bigger than
anything out there
in the world

bigger than

anything
the mind can
comprehend
and all that
inside
your own self
in a place
so small
it
isn't there.

Judevine Mountain Built a House

Judevine Mountain built a house on Judevine Mountain.
Six doors and windows let the world in, two other openings

let the refuse out. A woodstove heats the place. It keeps him
warm in the winter. He cooks his food and eats and sleeps

in there. He built the house himself, sturdily and well. But,
nonetheless, it's only a temporary shelter. Already it's falling

apart. Pretty soon it'll be completely gone, fallen back into
the ground, and Judevine Mountain gone, too. And then:

nothing left on Judevine Mountain but Judevine Mountain.

Perched in These Green Mountains

Han Shan says, *Perched in these green mountains,*
letting my hair grow white, pleased with the years gone by,
happy with today.

Imagine such contentment, happiness with yourself.
Yet I know for Cold Mountain, tomorrow always brought
something else as well, for Han Shan also said,

If you hide yourself away in the thickest woods,
how will your wisdom's light shine through?
A bag of bones is not a sturdy vessel.

Back and forth, back and forth.
That's the way it goes.
Happy and content one day,

ambition and desire eat you alive the next.
It's always been this way. Back and forth,
back and forth. That's the way it goes.

I've Got My Father's Ashes on My Desk

I've got my father's ashes on my desk
in a little brass urn so I can look at them
every morning before I start my work, so
I can pick them up and shake them, hear
what's left of him rattle around in there,
the larger pieces of bone and tooth clacking
against the side of that little brass urn.

All those pictures of Christian or Buddhist
monks—not just Saint Jerome—staring at
a human skull, looking deeply into those
hollows where two eyes once were, those
openings where a nose was, staring at what
stained teeth remain. All those monks over
all those years looking at The Skull
while it stares back and grins.

The First, the Greatest, the Best

Must we all die like the philosophy professor
      at the little college in Ohio
forever wishing he were somewhere else
      and hating himself for never
having really made it, for always being
      only second place?

To see the Ten Thousand Things clearly, distinctly,
      see each separate from the other,
and also simultaneously see each without distinction
      from the other
takes a lifetime of self-discipline and modesty,
      which is why, I think,
Taoists recluse themselves and live in quiet poverty.

To live in this world is to live with awards and prizes.
      Why do we always have to
line up according to ability? And who is to judge
      how that line should go?

This lust to be the first, the greatest, the best, makes either
      enemies or hypocrites of us all.
These distinctions make only jealousy and envy. They set
      our teeth on edge and us against one another.

All This Striving to Succeed
Will Make You a Failure for Sure

Win a prize:
      lose your life.
Get an honor:
      become dishonorable.

Why should a bag of bones
      what makes piss and shit
get all dolled up
      in all these honors?

I guess that's the reason.

What Is Ambition Compared to Death?

Confucius stood beside a river
        and sighed,
We pass on like this,
            never stopping day or night!

What could be more important
        than this life—
our days here
        on the earth?

What could be more important
        than the end
of this life toward which
        we all hurry?

What is ambition
        compared to death?
How can greed compete
        with our own dying?

Kim Ku-yong Says

Do not regret that you have
neither wealth nor fame;
Don't wind and moon
follow wherever you go?

Yeah, that's right, say I,
with such a following
who could ask
for anything more?

All This Ego

All this ego
all this drive
to get somewhere
when
at the finish line
death sits

one leg
over the other
hands folded
in his lap
a little smirk
on his face.

A Dream

I had a dream last night that—like Han Shan—
I'd left my wife and gone to live alone on
Judevine Mountain. Then, after thirty-five years,
I returned to my old home to see my wife.

> When I came into the house, she looked up
> from her newspaper. Her blank stare looked
> right through me, as if I weren't there. I turned
> and left without a word, returned to my

bitter loneliness up here on Judevine Mountain.
Then I woke up, reached over, wrapped my arms
and legs around my wife lying there beside me
and whispered to her sleeping form:

> *Thank you, oh thank you, for coming*
> *here with me all those many years ago.*

Gandhi Said Once

it took a thousand people
and a million dollars
to keep him in his poverty.

Okay. I'll tell the truth for once.
I couldn't dawdle away my life
watching birds and sky,

playing flutes and making poems
about how poor I am, if it weren't
for somebody else's money.

November Again Again

Gray, damp, sere, chill,
bare November days
here again this year.

Day after day
clouds down
around our ankles.

The quiet, meditative
beauty of these
muffled days.

Withdraw, return,
pull in,
to somewhere

inside
both house
and life.

Just Now

Dark falling fast and just now up the hill
    from where I write this
    deep in the woods, deep
in the hemlock thicket on the leeward side
    of the hill away from
    the cold west wind
a deer turns and turns around and around
    making her snowy bed
    into which now she lays
herself down, curls and tucks herself
    in upon herself
    then sinks into
a wakeful sleep in which she also
    listens for the
    approaching dogs.

End of November

Deer season over.
Deer hunters gone.

    Fewer and fewer people pass by
    on the road below the house.

Snow begins to fall here
on Judevine Mountain—

    a blanket
    for my garden.

In white quiet,
emptiness grows—

    this unseen winter vegetable
    fertilized by snow.

Part Three

Winter Is the Best Time

Winter is the best time
to find out who you are.

Quiet, contemplation time,
away from the rushing world,

cold time, dark time, holed-up,
pulled-in time and space

to see that inner landscape,
that place hidden and within.

The Mind No-Mind Brought to Mind

No reading. No thought.
No mind today.
Just eyes and ears,
nose and touch,
reaching out
into the world,
this world, out there
beyond me,
nothing to do with me,
alive and well and
going on
without me,
not caring anything
about me,
benign, indifferent, sweet—
and out there.
Alive and
nothing, nothing
to do with me.

Yang Wan-li Says

What a laugh!
All my theories are wrong!
I throw the book down
beside my pillow.

Oh, brother!
ain't it the truth.
What's enlightenment
got to do with mind?

I pick up my flute,
blow a few notes
and stare
out the window.

Same Old Thing

In the sixteenth century
Nobutada drew
with ink and brush on paper a picture of
a meditating Daruma
and to the left he brushed a poem:
> *Quietness and emptiness are enough*
> *to pass through life without error.*

Oh my, I've heard that song before:
Matthew 5:48—
> *Be ye therefore perfect, even as*
> *your Father which is in heaven is perfect.*

Emptiness? Perfection? Life without error?
> *Vanity of vanities; all is vanity.*

Straight like Iron

Han Shan says,
A real man's will is straight like iron.
In an uncrooked heart the Way is true.

Yeah, yeah, and *Strait* is *the gate, and narrow*
is *the way, which leadeth unto life, and few*
there be that find it, and so on and so on.

So who wants to be a real man anyway?

The Emperor

Lao Tzu said *flexibility and resilience* are what it takes to stay alive.
And *kindness,* Confucius believed, is the highest virtue.

So why is the Emperor so spiteful and malicious? Why
does he go around beating up on everybody all the time?

Why do so many people have to suffer and die just because
the Emperor and his Imperial Court have an idea?

Easy as Pie

The Emperor divides the world
into two parts:
the Good and the Evil.

If you don't accept that,
the Emperor says
you are Evil.

The Emperor declares himself
and his friends:
Good.

The Emperor says as soon as
Good has destroyed Evil,
all will be Good.

Simple as one, two, three.
Clear as night and day.
Different as black and white.

Easy as pie.

The Warrior's Question

How do you go into battle
wield the warrior's sword
cut off the dragon's head
and do it without any self?

If a Bodhisattva

If a Bodhisattva is one who, although enlightened,
chooses to remain here in this suffering world and

be with the Suffering People, then there is no escape
for any of us, since how could we gain enlightenment

by running away from the pain and injustice that are
all around us? To decide simply to remove yourself

from the fray, to sit down and find peace at the center
of a storm by ignoring the causes of that storm can't

possibly be a way to any understanding, for if such is
impossible for a Bodhisattva how much more impossible

for the temporal and worldly likes of you and me?

February 13, 2003

This evening on the radio
the Emperor said that he

had not yet decided
to order a war—

as if ordering a war
were something like

ordering a pizza.

It's Different Now

Chuang Tzu refused the offer of jade and gold
to come to the capital and advise the emperor.

Han Shan says he did the same thing. Those guys had iron wills.
Nothing could get them out of their woods and mountains.

I don't need to be so resolute since no emperor of mine
would ever imagine inviting me to town.

Reading Olav Hauge in the Dead of Winter

The winter is too long and drear.
I dream of spring, of light and air
that are warm and bright and clear.

Then suddenly to my reading eye
appears
Olav Hauge, and I hear him say,

The old poet has made a line.
And he's happy, happy as a cider bottle
in spring after it's sent
a fresh bubble up
and is about to pop its cork.

Yes, my old,
like-me-wannabe-Chinese, Norwegian friend,
to make a line
is almost as good
as spring.

Two Views of the Same Place

People say, *Oh! it must be so relaxing*
to live up there on your mountainside.
People say, *It's so laid-back up there.*

Yeah, well, it's off to The City for me
when I want to find some relaxation.
I wander the crowded streets, ride

the subway, eat exotic food, and
for a moment flee these thousand
thousand mountain cares.

Leaving Home

Farewell beautiful little house we built ourselves.
Farewell beautiful little house in the mountains.

Farewell woodstove that keeps us warm all winter.
Farewell beautiful little house with a lovely garden

just beyond the white pine tree. Farewell lovely garden
sleeping quietly now under the snow. Farewell snowy

mountainside. Farewell chickadees and blue jays,
grosbeaks and nuthatches. Farewell quiet. Farewell

solitude. I am bound for The City. Away! I am away!
I will return. I will return. I will return.

The Woodcutter

In ancient times
it was the woodcutter who knew
both the mountains and the city.

He lived and worked in one,
visited and sold in the other.
I'm the new woodcutter of old,

versed in the ways of both the country and the city,
content to spend my days alone in the forest
cutting, splitting, stacking firewood and boiling tea
over an open fire or riding the subway and wandering
the crammed and noisy streets of Chinatown,
lost in that crush and press of flesh.

I love both
the silence of the mountains
and the cacophony of the city.

Sounds and silence.
Crowds and emptiness.
Yang and yin.

What Would I Do Without Her?
or
The Hypocrite Tells the Truth for Once

I play my flutes and write my poems
about my purity and solitude
up here on Judevine Mountain

while she balances the checkbook
and worries about where the next
dollar is coming from while I play

my flutes and write my poems
about my purity and solitude
up here on Judevine Mountain.

Another Winter Night

Outside the wind howls,
the snow blows, the temperature's
below zero. Here inside

the room is warm, the candles make a glow,
the woodstove ticks, the teapot sings
an almost-not-there song.

We eat our dinner on the couch
pressed up against each other:
rice and dal and warm chapatis,

then stretch out and each take a corner
of the couch. I put my left foot high up
on the inside of her thigh.

Part Four

Thirty-five Years Alone

Thirty-five years alone at the foot of Judevine Mountain raising vegetables, cutting firewood, talking to the birds, and making poems hasn't exactly made Judevine Mountain a household word in the poetry academy.

Once a friend recommended him to the academy and they all cried, *Who's this Judevine Mountain guy?* Another friend—who just happened to be there—said, *Everybody in these parts knows who he is.*

Why, he's the most famous unknown poet for miles around. The only people around here who don't know who he is, is you! Which, of course, proved to the academy that he didn't exist at all. And therefore

Judevine Mountain was set free to continue on his mountainside raising vegetables, cutting firewood, talking to the birds, and making poems, which he is doing to this very day, in his nonexistent sort of way.

Well, Most of the Time Anyway

Most of the time
I can honestly say,
as Han Shan said,
Face brown, head white,
content with mountain life,
my beat-up chore coat on,
watch cap on my head,
out among my gardens—

I don't envy others.
I'm happy with my life.

Wild Monk Or?

Wild monk on far roads deep in the mountains
where nobody knows who you are, or known poet?

This world or the other?
This question of ambition.

What if I gave up my lust for fame and
disappeared? What if I wrote my poems

only on walls or scraps of paper
and gave them away to strangers?

What Is Going On Here?

Han Shan said, *Though*
I look down again on the
dusty world, what's that
land of dreams to me?

Chuang Tzu said,
If you're at peace...
sorrow and joy
can never touch you.

What the fuck
is going on here?
These guys are
talking corpses!

Do Something with Your Body

Yak. Yak. Yak.
All these intellectuals ever want to do is talk.
They think words will get them somewhere.

Why don't they take a hike or catch a fish
or cook a meal or cut and split some wood
or make love or dance?

Why don't they do something
with their bodies? Maybe then they'd
begin to know what to talk about,

the poet said as he sat there
talking to his paper.
Yak. Yak. Yak.

Dialogue

When the weeds are poking through your skull,
then there's plenty of time for regrets.
HAN SHAN

One voice says:
Why spend all your time chasing after money, things,
knowledge, wisdom? Don't you know it's all for naught?
You're just a bag of bones walking toward an early grave.

Another voice says:
Why detach yourself from life that way? Join the fray,
jump in, have a go at it while you've got the chance.
Don't hesitate. Play music, dance, and sing. Eat whatever
you want. And if you can't make love to someone every day,
make love to yourself. Don't worry about money.
You're only here a little while.

The Mountain Recluse Asks Himself a Question

I'm over sixty.

Am I old enough now
to let go of my
young-man,
white-knuckle
grip
on dreams
of fame and fortune,
travel,
strange and beautiful women
who follow me wherever I go?

Am I old enough?

Naw,
not yet.

The Beautiful People

He is young
       and handsome.
She is young
       and beautiful.
They are wealthy
       and intelligent.
Everything they turn
       their hands to
becomes
       a great success.

Maybe they will figure out
       how not to die.

Again Just Now

That gorgeous young woman
sashays down the street just now

full of her life and sex because
she can't imagine her white hair,

wrinkled skin, bent back, and
withered breasts, and I am glad

she can't. There's time enough later
for her old age. Just now her beautiful

ass swinging down the street
makes both our lives a pleasure.

He Grieves

He grieves to see his hair turn white
HAN SHAN

He grieves over thoughts of what might have been.
He grieves to see his flesh wrinkle and sag.
He grieves to see his flesh crumple and flake off.
He grieves at losing the power to attract women.
He grieves at not being able to do the things he once did.
He grieves every morning over how much his body hurts.
Such are the pains of a man growing old.

The World Left Behind

Those memories of
what never was:

who is strong enough,
wise enough,

not to look back, and
wonder over all those

other places, other lives
that might have been?

Ugly Americans

Question:
Americans climb all over the earth to get what they want.
They bomb anybody anywhere anytime if they feel like it.
And all that just to get some more oil or bauxite or human chattel
to make more gas or plastic or aluminum or sneakers or cars.

What causes all this pride, this hubris, all this greed?
How come we assume the entire world is ours to pillage?
Why do we just automatically presume that every poor person
in the world was born to be our servant?
Where did we get these ideas?

Answer:
March 1640, a town in the Massachusetts Bay Colony,
the annual town meeting: from the minutes:

Resolved: that the earth is the Lord's
and the followers thereof.
It was so voted.

Resolved: that the Lord may give the earth or any part of it
to his chosen people.
It was so voted.

Resolved: that we
are his chosen people.
It was so voted.

The Rich Are Never Satisfied

It should be plain for all to see,
wealth is the mother of greed.

Han Shan says the rich are never satisfied.
No matter how much they have it's never enough.

Han Shan says they're stingy too. Even when they've got
a granary full of stale rice, they won't loan out a peck.

It's still that way. The Emperor's richer than an emperor,
yet all he wants to do is take money from the poor and give

it to himself and his rich friends. The more those people
have the more they want. They'll never have enough.

Here and There:
A Sunny Day, April 2003

Imagine your body on fire.
Imagine your arms blown away.

Imagine your hands off there somewhere
lying around on the lawn.

Imagine your body in pieces
scattered across the street.

Imagine yourself crawling around
trying to find your feet.

I imagine all this as I whiz down the highway
my latte by my side while public radio plays

some Telemann music and I hear the
announcer say, "Oh! what a beautiful day."

Sympathy for the Poor

Just because you have what you want today
doesn't mean you will tomorrow.

On a whim you could be homeless, on the street,
out there in the cold and wind.

Better you should have some sympathy for the poor,
since you might be one of them tomorrow.

April 3, 2003

The end of winter: evening falling.
Outside: the world is mud and rotten snow.
Inside: a little fire in the woodstove takes the chill away.
The kitchen: warm and comfortable.
Pasta, red sauce, wine, and salad.
Some tinkling sounds in the evening glow.

After supper we lie together wrapped around each other
in the quiet evening, in the peaceful dark, the sweet silence.

What else is there to want except supper together,
a place to lie down and hold each other?

Half a world away, Dr. Saad al-Fallouji, the hospital's chief surgeon, said
that just today the hospital received 33 victims dead on arrival
and 180 others who were wounded by American fire.

All of them were civilians, he said. *All of them were from Nadir village,
women and children and men of all ages, mostly they had very serious
injuries to their abdomens, to their intestines, to their chests and their heads.
Many of the bodies were completely torn apart,* he said.

Love Song

See how when she holds her arm out straight and she is not
wearing a shirt—see how the flesh under her upper arm
where her triceps is or was—how it hangs loose and flaps as
she moves her arm—how the flesh hangs loose off the bone,

looser and looser off the bone each year as she gets older—
and see how the sides of his face, his jowls, sag more each year,
and the flesh where his arm meets his chest, that muscle that
used to be his breast—how it sags too and how also what was

once his high, tight, firm ass—how it sags more and more
each year. See how the wrinkles, lines, bags in their faces,
on their backs and legs increase as the years go by—how
for both of them the flesh falls slowly away from

muscle, tendon, bone—how it increasingly falls away
as they become visions of the death they move toward.

Another Spring

I'm at work in the vegetable garden raking the freshly turned soil,
she in the dooryard tending her mother's irises, which only
in the last few days have appeared above the ground.

The birds who stay with us all winter sing their springtime songs,
and the geese go north above us. Another spring
and everything is young again but us.

I see her there bending over the flower bed. Her hair is gray.
She moves more slowly, rests more often.
I look and do the same.

Where is renewal for us?
Where is our youth?
Why can't we be young again also?

Birth and Death in the Dooryard

For two weeks we watched
as mother downy woodpecker

fed her young. Then today
under the apple tree I found

the rotting corpse of her child,
already insects crawling on it,

a clear liquid oozing from
its breast, its eyes a dull blue-gray

and sinking back into its head
as all of it sinks back into earth.

In the Year in Which I Was Fifty-seven

My father is ninety-one years old.
He lies in a bed in a nursing home
naked except for his diaper.

He has one leg,
one eye, no teeth,
and he's deaf.

I wish he would die
so my future
wouldn't be so clear.

Written While Riding the Q Train across
Manhattan Bridge into Chinatown in a City
I Once Called Home
             or
    Self-Pity in the City

Leave the city. Go to the mountains.
Live your life. Make your poems.
What good does it do
if no one ever reads them?

Thirty-five years go by and old age
stares you in the face. Yet you know
your heart and passion grow stronger,
more urgent, every day. You know
you are better than you've ever been.

What good does all that do
if nobody knows where you are?

Look at Her Now

That gorgeous young woman I saw on the subway
last night, the one with the round, erect breasts,

and sweet delicate arms and high fine ass, and oh!
those hips, those sleek legs and thin ankles, those eyes,

those lips, her smile, the way her hair fell away from
her graceful neck so gracefully...

Han Shan says in thirty years that beautiful young
thing will look *like chewed sugarcane.* He says

in thirty years she'll look like me. Yes, Han Shan, yes.
But who cares? It's now. Now. Just look at her now!

Now Look at Me

As Ryōkan said once:
I was away in the calm
of a mountain retreat
just yesterday.

Now look at me!
I've spent all night listening to wild,
ecstatic jazz, this Sacred Black Music.

It's four in the morning and here I am
at the Odessa on Avenue A and Eighth Street,
eating potato pancakes and applesauce
and talking and laughing with friends.

Walking down the street now
with morning dawning over Brooklyn,
I sing praises to the gods
for this my fortunate life.

Going Home

Farewell noisy, dirty, gross, wonderful, exciting, vibrant, pulsing city.
Farewell Russell from Trinidad and Andrei from Bedford-Stuyvesant.
Farewell coconut drops from the Jamaican bakery.
Farewell roti from the roti shack on Flatbush Avenue.
Farewell Anna and J from Brooklyn.
Farewell Matt and Audra from the Upper West Side.
Farewell William and Patricia from the East Village.
Farewell Nadine and Shalini from the corner of Ocean and Parkside.
Farewell Grand Sichuan Restaurant and that whole fish—head and tail
and bulging eyes and all—deboned, rolled in flour, turned inside out,
deep-fried and then smothered in a sweet pine-nut sauce—that we ate.
Farewell sautéed lightly, deep, brilliant green, Chinese greens.
Farewell blazing hot, take-the-top-of-your-head-off pork dish.
Farewell delicate and mild scallop and Chinese cucumber dish.
Farewell tea.
Farewell friendly couple who run the restaurant.
Farewell the best food anybody could ever eat.
Farewell Q train rumbling over the Manhattan Bridge at night.
Farewell lights of lower Manhattan glittering in the night.
Farewell Brooklyn Bridge and Statue of Liberty glittering in the night.
Farewell horns and blare and crowds and lights and noise.
Farewell. Farewell. I'm bound back home to solitude and silence.
Away! I am away! I will return. I will return. I will return.

Judevine Mountain's Siren Song:
Upon Returning Home from the City

When she speaks her voice is like singing.
Her song is an intoxication.
She beckons to me to come near.
She asks me to stay until morning comes.
Her bed is large and comfortable.
The sheets are sweet smelling and clean.
Many fine and colorful quilts wait to cover us both.

How can I turn away from her open arms?
How can I resist her welcoming bower?

Part Five

What It Takes

Enough
of a house
to keep
the bugs and rain
out
in the summer,
stay warm
in
in the winter.

Books,
a few
musical instruments,
a garden,
silence,
some mountains,

maybe a cat.

Summer's Here

Summer's here and we can hike the peaks again,
have lunch and tea on mountaintops, look down

on the backs of circling hawks and laze away
the afternoon watching blue-hazy, distant hills.

Come on! Give up those winter blues. Let's go!
Grease up those boots, find that walking stick.

Get your lungs and legs in shape. And don't forget
what Yüan Mei said, two hundred years ago:

If you begrudge your feet some pain
you'll miss ten thousand peaks.

Don't Speak in the Abstract

Say rather:
It's a nice day.
Pass the mashed potatoes, please.
Look, there's a chickadee.
Your voice makes me swoon.
Let's plant the beans.
I miss my dead mother so much today.
I want to touch your face.
Clean up this mess!
What's better than a cool glass of water?
I feel so sad; all I want to do is cry.
What time is it?
I want to touch you everywhere.
Let's go for a walk.
Will you have tea with me?
Let's play some music.
I don't want to die.
Come visit again soon.

Praise for Ambition and Lust

We rise out of the undifferentiated Tao like bean plants
    emerging from the garden's soil.

For a moment we are here under the summer rain and sun,
    alive, in love with now.

And because we are, the pests of Ambition and Lust
    attack us.

Yet, if we were not here to be attacked,
    where would we be?

Without the struggle what is there?
    So let us now sing praises to

Ambition and Lust.
    These proofs we are alive.

After a Painting by Tu Chin Called
The Scholar Fu Sheng in a Garden

Here is Fu Sheng wizened, bald, old, wrinkled and skinny,
leaning on his staff, next to the young woman, whose body
is smooth and round, her hair black, her robes full of her
young flesh that we know under those robes is delicate
and beautiful, and oh, oh, oh, oh so wonderful to touch.

Fu Sheng looks sideways toward the young woman.
She looks demurely away. And with that gaze of envy
and longing, old Fu Sheng draws out of her lithe and
succulent body her enthusiasm and energy so that he
can keep himself going a little longer.

With Hui-neng

I'm no monk, that's for sure.
I like this life, our flesh too much
to want to find a way away from it.

With Hui-neng, I say, *To still*
the mind and contemplate purity
is a disease, not meditation.

Contemplation of the thing
or the thing itself?
Which one would you choose?

As Mr. Cummings used to say,
a pretty girl who naked is
is worth a million statues.

The Old Tree

The old tree is gnarled and wounded,
    scarred and deformed—

made beautiful, people say, by age,
    experience, long-suffering.

Why then do the beautiful and young
    turn away from the old?

Why do they want only the smooth and tender,
    the succulent and pliable?

The Way Is like Language

The Way is like language. The more you use it,
the more it responds, becomes resilient, pliable,
lithe, liquid, smooth, supple, available, eager.

Go ahead, do anything you want to it. You can't
hurt it. It is far more powerful than you are.
It's there to serve and dominate you all at once.

Surrender to it and it will be your servant.
It is your tool, your toy, your master.

No Escape

Nineteen sixty-eight was a hell of a year.
Riots, assassinations, wars, *mere anarchy*—
as W.B. Yeats said—loosed upon the streets.

I hung in there as long as I could, endured bedlam
on the ship of state as long as possible, and then
on a summer day in 1969—at the age of twenty-nine—
I jumped overboard and swam all the way up here
to Judevine Mountain, to where I thought I might,
as Han Shan said, *dwell and gaze in freedom.*

It's thirty-five years later now and still I know
it is impossible to leave my country. Even though
I live among these cliffs hidden by the clouds,
there is still nowhere I can hide from the way
the Emperor and his Court beat up on the world.

Litany for the Emperor

I don't want to fight your war.
      I want to make   applesauce.
I don't want to fight your war.
      I want to make   the bed.
I don't want to fight your war.
      I want to make   cookies.
I don't want to fight your war.
      I want to make   love.
I don't want to fight your war.
      I want to make   it over to my friend's house.
I don't want to fight your war.
      I want to make   a poem.
I don't want to fight your war.
      I want to make   it to work tomorrow.
I don't want to fight your war.
      I want to make   a salad.

Where I Went to School

I came here thirty-five years ago to escape the sophistication and
the arrogance of the literati, to hide among these mountains,
to live a simple life connected to the seasons, to raise vegetables,
cut wood, and listen for a poem to wander by singing its song.

My neighbors, what few there were, were simple farmers who
wore plain clothes and smelled like earth and cow manure.
The cycle of birth, youth, old age, and death ruled their lives
every day in the barn, chicken coop, pigpen, garden, bedroom.

In their dealings with me they were both straightforward and shy.
They said what they thought. They knew nothing of deception and
had no idea what flattery was. I lived among them and went about
my own business as they did theirs. They were my writing teachers.

This is where I went to school.

The Evolution of Soph

Sophist.
Sophistry.
Sophomore.
Sophisticated.

When Han Shan Was Twenty-nine

When Han Shan was twenty-nine
he left his family and friends and
went to live alone on Cold Mountain.

How could he do that?
How could he be so alone?
He must have been an unhappy guy.

What good is enlightenment
without your family and friends?

Questions

Did Han Shan run away from life?
From his family, from his children and his wife,
so that he could avoid this world and its attachments?

And if he did—what's so admirable about that?

Did I come here to this lonely mountainside
all those years ago also at the tender age of twenty-nine
to hide from the world? Was I just afraid
to jump into the Great Competition? Was I
afraid of failing at a job, falling in love with
someone else, getting in trouble with a student
at a college somewhere, making a fool of myself
in some other way?

Or was I looking for some other way to live my life?

My Father Is with Me

I am sixty-four years old, but I still can ride a bike
over logging roads, up mountains, down into valleys,
ten or fifteen miles without stopping; sweating,
cardiovascular pump banging away, and
I feel good, damn good, and so on.

I could go on bragging, and I will too,
some other time, because:

I carry with me on those rides the memory
of my father before he died, this memory that
is a vision also of myself, sometime not too far off
in the future, when I will take his place, and it is I
lying in a bed, alone and lonely in a nursing home,
shitting in my diaper, one leg, one eye, no teeth, and deaf.

So I ride on and on, doing everything I can to postpone
that time when I take my father's place.

The Circle Is Unbroken

I saw an old man
      staggering down the street today,
ashen, unshaven,

his arms leaning and shaking
      on his walker
as he shuffled along.

I saw my father,
      dead now these few years.
I saw myself.

Ryōkan Says

With what can I
compare this life?
        Weeds floating on water.

And there you are with your
dreams of immortality
        through poetry.

Pretty pompous—
don't you think?—for a
        weed floating on water?

Lies

Who you are and who
      you think you are
are almost never the same.
      Wang Wei
the ex–government official
      seeking in his
retirement the solitude and
      silence of his
Buddhist faith referred to his
      retreat on the
Wang River as a shack. It was
      a palatial estate
with servants everywhere.
      He was a rich guy.

I call myself a recluse yet
      I run around
almost as much as anyone.

Poets never tell the truth.

Walking Meditation

Chia Tao says
walking meditation
drives out thoughts
of fame and fortune.

Chia Tao says
walking meditation
stills the ego-mad mind.

I walk and walk
but it doesn't do any good.
My ego-mad mind
dreams on and on.

Glad to Be Who They Are

Just think of what a good time we could have,
how much of the world we could notice and enjoy,
if we were happy to be who we are.

Year after year the loons return to Judevine Mountain Pond.
They nest, brood, hatch and raise their young—two of them,
almost every year. They seem happy with what they have and
where they are. They don't want more and more all the time.
They seem glad to be who they are, doing what they do:
raising young, fishing, swimming, flying around and hollering.

The last lines of chapter 81 of
Lao Tzu's *Tao Te Ching* say:

Their food is plain and good, and they enjoy eating it.
Their clothes are simple and beautiful.
Their homes secure.
They are happy in their ways.
Though they live within sight of their neighbors,
and their chickens and dogs call back and forth,
they leave one another in peace as they all grow old and die.

My Father

My father was a city kid who grew up on the streets
    and in the alleys of Cleveland, Ohio.

All his life he had a dream of going to the country,
    going to the country to be free.

He never broke away. I did it for him, and came
    up here to Judevine Mountain.

Before my father died, he'd visit here and sit in the
    dooryard underneath the apple tree

on a summer afternoon with his baby granddaughter
    on his lap and look out at the gardens

and to the mountains beyond and say,
    You really got it, Bud. You really got it.

Like Smoke from Our Campfire

All those plans for fame and fortune, honor and glory,
    where are they now?

Drifted away like smoke from our campfire, dissipated
    into the thin, night air,

the fire deserted and gone down to a few ashy coals,
    almost out.

And all of those who sat around the fire: gone away too
    into oblivion.

Too Busy

Have ambition and ego ruined my life?
Where have my easy days gone?

If only I had a monk friend off there in
the mountains somewhere. If only I were
so idle I had time to visit him. If only we
could while away the day drinking tea,
playing flutes, and talking. If only, as the
moon rose, my friend could point the way
home through the dark mountains with
only the night sky's lantern to light the way.

If only I were happy with only that.

The Busy Man Speaks

Appointments, schedules, deadlines.
Demands on my time from everywhere.
I've got to plan every minute.

I'm so busy I don't have time to
trust the current like an unmoored boat.

I wouldn't want to anyway.
I make the current go
where *I* want it to go.
I'm in charge here.

Poem with a Quotation from Mr. Lin

On a summer day in 1969, at the age of twenty-nine, having known riots,
assassinations, wars, and mere anarchy loosed upon the streets,
I gave up life in the world of red dust and exiled myself into
these mountains thinking I might find here a more civil, decent,
kind, human, and humane way to live my life. I was looking
for what Mr. Lin dreamed of out loud one summer day in 1944
on a tea plantation in the Wu-i Mountains of Fukien—a time
of war and pestilence in his land also:

> *All this peace and quiet… sparkling water, mountain food, up early*
> *in the morning when the birdsong grows clamorous, forest walks,*
> *kindly people, friendly animals unafraid of people, a neighbor or two,*
> *…a cottage with some books and a couple of musical instruments.*
> *One could live like those scholars of old who, retiring before the age*
> *of thirty, entered the Way and became Immortals.*

Well, no immortality for me: just thirty-five years on the Way,
a balding head, the constant struggle, the daily rounds, pleasures,
and regrets, and thirty-five years closer to my own death. And now

war again—
naked power, carnage, greed,
hubris, ideology—
again.

Of Two Minds

As Ryōkan said,
Truly I love this life of seclusion.

Then why do I pine away
for a visit from friends?

And why,
when they do come,

why is it
all I can think about

is how to get away,
get back into the woods,

back to my life
of seclusion?

Green Mountain Woodchuck Landscape Haiku

Dirt roads, power lines,
chicken coop, dead cars, trailer—
mountains all around.

Right Now

Right now there's an evening grosbeak
perched on the topmost branch of the
fifty-foot-high white pine tree
here on the edge of the dooryard.

Oh, how I'd like to be up there!

How I would like to see what my house
and gardens look like from up there
and the woods around here
and the mountains far away.

Often I Think I'd Rather

                play my flute than write a poem—
those pure or impure tones
                going out into the air,
those runs or stumbles
                up and down some scale,
no need for thought,
                no need for wisdom,
nothing for the mind to do,
                just emotion, feeling, sound,
traveling on my breath
                coming up and out of me
and through the flute,
                directly out of me,
directly into you,
                my breath saying all
that need be said
                by saying nothing at all.

The End of August

I am overtired
Of the great harvest I myself desired.
ROBERT FROST

It's the end of August and I'm tired.
The garden is tired. The grass is tired.

Everything is tired. We've all had
too much summer.

Bring on the cold. Bring on the frost.
Bring on all that death and destruction.

Let's have some quiet and some peace.
Let us rest. Give us emptiness.

Part Six

After Looking at an Anonymous
Sung-Dynasty Painting Called
Lake Retreat among Willow Trees

In this Chinese painting from a thousand years ago,
two figures at a rustic lakeside cottage sit outdoors
under a lattice, across a table from each other with tea,
engaged in conversation.

Summer turning toward fall, these two friends
by the water, reclusion, a visit, profound discussion
of the Tao or maybe only lighthearted jokes
about politicians or no talking at all.

Only the sound of wind across water,
a slight rustle as it moves through
the overhanging willow trees, their leaves
now beginning to yellow.

Two figures, caught here in this painting, forever,
free of war, free of worry, enjoying the late summer air,
their friendship, the tea, a slight breeze.

A Little Story about an
Ancient Chinese Emperor

Thousands of years ago in ancient China a boy emperor ruled for a while.
The Imperial Court had placed the child on the throne so that he could be
a mouthpiece for the Imperial Court's desires.

Coddled from birth, surrounded by servants and sycophants,
told by the Imperial Court that he was the Son of Heaven,
given to believe he had no obligation to anyone but his Imperial Court,
pampered and protected from any notion of what the real world was like,
from any idea of what the People had to put up with every day,

the Emperor stomped and swaggered through the world
telling the People what to do, taking whatever he wanted,
robbing from the poor and giving to the rich, and sending
his armies out to terrorize whomever he took a notion to despise.

The Emperor ruled for a long time and thousands of the People
died, killed by his armies and because of his abuse and neglect.
But, eventually, after great suffering, the People rose up and
crushed the man who called himself the Son of Heaven.
And they crushed his Imperial Court as well.

Then some time passed in which the People lived in relative calm
until another Emperor, like the one in this story, came along.

Yellow Leaves—Red Leaves

Yellow leaves,
red leaves,
brown leaves,
    chrysanthemums,

and day and night

geese
pointing south
and crying:
    Good bye!

October Day—October Night

Orange light,
yellow light,
autumn light:

over the trails
on Judevine Mountain,
and home

through the noisy leaves.

Starry night,
moony night,
clear and bright,

and coyotes
yipping
into the cold.

The Lazy Bees

Twenty October
sunny
seventy degrees.

The lazy bees
doze
and feed

on the
chrysanthemums.

No Poems

Yellow leaves
      pile up
on the Scholar's
      inkstone.
His brush
      is dry.

He lies
      still as death
on his cot
      curled in
upon
      himself.

Gone away
      on his
autumnal
      wander
through
      Depression.

This Shining Moment in the Now

When I work outdoors all day, every day, as I do now, in the fall,
getting ready for winter, tearing up the garden, digging potatoes,
gathering the squash, cutting firewood, making kindling, repairing
bridges over the brook, clearing trails in the woods, doing the last of
the fall mowing, pruning apple trees, taking down the screens,
putting up the storm windows, banking the house—all these things,
as preparation for the coming cold...

when I am every day all day all body and no mind, when I am
physically, wholly and completely in this world with the birds,
the deer, the sky, the wind, the trees...

when day after day I think of nothing but what the next chore is,
when I go from clearing woods roads to sharpening a chain saw,
to changing the oil in a mower, to stacking wood, when I am
all body and no mind...

when I am only here and now and nowhere else—then, and only
then, do I see the crippling power of mind, the curse of thought,
and I pause and wonder why I so seldom find
this shining moment in the now.

My Old and Well-Known Lover

In autumn the world lets fall
all the garments of summer:
      heat, people, birds, leaves.

And I awake one day to see
my old and well-known lover
      standing there naked shivering

in nothing but her cloudy robe.

A Nameless Ghost

Han Shan says, *Death makes you
a nameless ghost.* What good will come
of all your striving?

Yet we go on struggling to be known. Why
all this writing to overcome what cannot be
overcome? What good will it all do?

Will your poems seduce a dark young maiden
when you are underground? And even if they do,
what good is that to you

when you are just a jar of ashes?

All Ye Who Are Doubtful and Confused

Take heart, rejoice! all Ye
who are doubtful and confused.

Jesus said:
> *Unless you turn and become like children,*
> *you will never enter the kingdom of heaven.*

Lao Tzu said:
> *I alone seem to have nothing. I'm a man*
> *with the mind of an idiot, a pure fool. I'm*
> *dull and stupid. I never know what I'm doing.*

John Coltrane said:
> *I don't know. I'm searching.*

Chuang Tzu said:
> *A sage steers by the bright light of confusion and doubt.*

Carnal Vision

My carnal vision
never goes away.
My love, my lust—

for life, our flesh,
is always here.

Food, music, sex,
the delights of eye,
ear, nose, and fingertips—

it's how I know
I am alive.

A Question

Who would want
to discover
the jewel of our mind
and reach nirvana
and step off this
never-ending wheel
and not be able to
come back again
to know more love
and suffering?

What's so great
about
being nothing?

Envoi to a Question

Well, if you've known more love than suffering,
there's nothing so great about being nothing,

but if what you've known is what Buddha said,
that *life is suffering,* then what could be better

than to discover *the jewel of our mind,* to cross the
River Jordan to Beulah Land, and find eternal rest?

That Rebellious Streak Always Did Him In

Han Shan never could
        get into officialdom.
Maybe it was his bum leg,
        or maybe, more likely,
his rebellious attitude toward
        the doctrinal rigidity
of the exams. And he certainly
        revolted constantly
against the religious orthodoxies
        of his time.

He just never was able
        to do things
the way they were supposed
        to be done.

That rebellious streak always
        did him in,
and, without the imprimatur of
        a sinecure, there
never was much recognition or food
        on the table.

It was his fate. He couldn't be
        any other way.

A Cave on Judevine Mountain

There is a cave on Judevine Mountain, a secret place,
way back in the woods, high up on a hidden slope,

in a place no one ever goes. Only I know where it is.
No one else has ever been there. I go up there a lot

and sit around, make a little fire, boil some tea,
sometimes cook a little meal, but mostly what I do is

sit and wait, poke at the fire, add a twig or two
and wait and wait and stare, until suddenly

I know what to do.

Learning Patience

Again and again
when I was young
and in church I
heard the preacher
say:

Wait on the Lord:
be of good courage,
and he shall strengthen
thine heart: wait, I say,
on the Lord.

The Woodcutter Changes His Mind

When I was young, I cut the bigger, older trees for firewood, the ones
with heart rot, dead and broken branches, the crippled and deformed

ones, because, I reasoned, they were going to fall soon anyway, and
therefore, I should give the younger trees more light and room to grow.

Now I'm older and I cut the younger, strong and sturdy, solid
and beautiful trees, and I let the older ones have a few more years

of light and water and leaf in the forest they have known so long.
Soon enough they will be prostrate on the ground.

What Good Is This?

What good is this life
of contemplation
and withdrawal?

It just makes you
more aware
of the passing years,
more sensitive to
old age and death.

Too much grief
and melancholy
makes you old
before your time.

It's Now or Never

Eat, drink, and be merry, for
tomorrow you will surely die.

Get together with your friends.
Enjoy the pleasures of the flesh.

I'm pretty sure this is all we get.
I can't be absolutely certain, but

of all the people I have known who
have passed over to the other side

not one has sent back any news.

Unnamed in the Records of Immortals

Up here in what looks like the wilderness,
    way out in the deepest woods,
there are old cellar holes: all that's left of houses
    from long ago.

And the names of those
    who lived there,
the stories of what they did
    are long gone also.

Someday someone may come by here and wonder
    what *common bones*
unnamed in the records of immortals
    lived here as well.

My House

I built the house I live in.
I built it myself.
It's been sturdy and strong all these years.
Now little by little something cracks here, breaks there,
falls apart somewhere else.

Repair this. Fix that.
It's an endless and losing battle.
It can't last forever no matter how hard I work at it.
After a while you just can't keep up.
Sooner or later it's going to come down.

Making a Poem by Quoting Issa

I am old enough for frosty hair.
The years add wrinkles to my face.

Life is brief; desire infinite.
I, too, am made of dust.

This world of dew
is only the world of dew—

and yet…
Oh! and yet…

Part Seven

What We Need

The Emperor,
his bullies
and henchmen
terrorize the world
every day,

which is why
every day

we need

a little poem
of kindness,

a small song
of peace

a brief moment
of joy.

What Have I Got to Complain About?

We've got enough money now not to worry every minute
about where the next dollar is coming from.
We even go to the movies once in a while.
We've got a nice collection of friends.
Our house is sturdy and well built.
It keeps us warm and stands well against the storms.
The larder is full of rice.
There are plenty of potatoes down cellar.
The freezer is full of vegetables I grew myself.

In the face of all of that, slights to my vanity
seem frivolous and nonsensical.

What have I got to complain about?

Different Names, the Same Person

More than a thousand years ago when I lived in China,
my name was Han Shan. And there were more of me
before that.

And plenty after also. Two hundred years ago,
in Japan, I called myself Ryōkan.
All of us:

independent, hating literary artifice and arrogance,
yet neither misanthropic nor taciturn,
friendly and talkative rather, but

preferring to live alone, in solitude, removed
and in the wilderness, keeping to that kind
of emptiness.

We've always been around, in lots of different places,
in every age. It's just, only some of us
get known.

There's one of us, I'm sure,
in your neighborhood
right now.

Winter: Tonight: Sunset

Tonight at sunset, walking on the snowy road,
my shoes crunching on the frozen gravel, first

through the woods, then out into the open fields
past a couple of trailers and some pickup trucks, I stop

and look at the sky. Suddenly: orange, red, pink, blue,
green, purple, yellow, gray, all at once and everywhere.

I pause in this moment at the beginning of my old age
and I say a prayer of gratitude for getting to this evening,

a prayer for being here, today, now, alive
in this life, in this evening, under this sky.

On the Other Side of Anger

On the other side of anger,
on the other side of ridicule and sarcasm,
beyond words:

an opening, a field
and in the center of the field
sitting on a stone:

a great sad beast
his head in his hands
weeping

for all of us.

South China Tiger,
Green Mountain Catamount

Big Stick,
Cold Mountain's friend,
rode around on a tiger.

When I reach enlightenment,
I'm riding out of here
on the back of the extinct
Green Mountain catamount.

Which means,
I hope it's a long time
before I meet
my four-legged taxi
to oblivion.

Tomorrow

Tomorrow
we are
bones and ash,
the roots of weeds
poking through
our skulls.

Today,
simple clothes,
empty mind,
full stomach,
alive, aware,
right here,
right now.

Drunk on music,
who needs wine?

Come on,
Sweetheart,
let's go dancing
while we've still
got feet.

Findings List and References

Many of these poems were inspired by reading other poets' poems. The ancient Chinese poets called this "harmonization." Here is a findings list for the Han Shan poems, the greatest influence here, that I have harmonized. I've read four different translations of Han Shan's poems. They are keyed as follows:

RP = Red Pine, *The Collected Songs of Cold Mountain*, Copper Canyon Press, 2000

BW = Burton Watson, *Cold Mountain: 100 Poems by the T'ang Poet Han-shan*, Columbia University Press, 1970

AT = Arthur Tobias, *The View from Cold Mountain*, White Pine Press, 1982

GS = Gary Snyder, *Riprap and Cold Mountain Poems*, Four Seasons Foundation, 1965

fn = indicates source is in a footnote at that location

Mixed among these Han Shan harmonizations are the other poets, poems, and sources referenced in this book.

EPIGRAPHS

Nessmuk (George W. Sears), *Woodcraft*, Dover Publications, 1963, p. 78.

Ryōkan, *The Zen Poems of Ryōkan*, trans. Nobuyuki Yuasa, Princeton University Press, 1981, p. 58.

joel oppenheimer, in conversation, circa 1985.

Ryōkan, my own version based on translations by Burton Watson, John Stevens, and Sam Hamill.

PART ONE

"Gama Sennin": cover illustration of this book, ink drawing by Soga Shōhaku (1730–1781), Freer Gallery of Art, Washington, D.C.

"Thirty-five Years": RP1&2, AT1&2, GS2.

"Drink a Cup of Loneliness": RP4, BW50, AT3, GS5.

"Thirty-five Miles to a Traffic Light": RP157, BW45, GS14.

"In the Tradition": RP3fn, BW48, GS1; T'ao Yüan-ming (aka T'ao Ch'ien), cf. Han-Shan Te-ch'ing section, *The Clouds Should Know Me by Now: Buddhist Poet Monks of China*, Red Pine and Mike O'Conner, eds. Wisdom Publications, 1998, pp. 122, 135 (fn10); also *Ryōkan: Zen Monk-Poet of Japan*, trans. Burton Watson, Columbia University Press, 1977, p. 33.

"Up Here": RP31, BW2.

"Directions": RP16, BW82, AT9, GS6.

"Irrelevant and Useless": RP11&12, AT7.

"Weather Report": RP16, BW82, AT9, GS6.

PART TWO

"Judevine Mountain Built a House": RP167, GS16.

"Perched in These Green Mountains": RP69, BW53, AT15&18; first quote from AT18, second quote from AT15.

"What Is Ambition Compared to Death?": RP53fn, BW85, GS10; quote from Confucius, *The Analects,* trans. David Hinton, Counterpoint, 1998, 9:17.

"Kim Ku-yong Says": *The Moonlit Pond: Korean Classical Poems in Chinese,* trans. Sung-Il Lee, Copper Canyon Press, 1998, p. 37.

"A Dream": RP43&137, BW63&83.

"Gandhi Said Once": RP133.

PART THREE

"Yang Wan-li Says": *Heaven My Blanket, Earth My Pillow: Poems from Sung Dynasty China by Yang Wan-li,* trans. Jonathan Chaves, Weatherhill, 1975, p. 69.

"Same Old Thing": Nobutada, *The Art of Zen,* by Stephen Addiss, Harry N. Abrams, 1989, pp. 20–23; Matthew 5:48, King James Version; "Vanity of vanities…," Ecclesiastes 1:2, King James Version.

"Straight like Iron": RP85; Matthew 7:14, King James Version.

"The Emperor": RP152.

"February 13, 2003": George Bush as quoted on National Public Radio's *All Things Considered,* February 13, 2003.

"It's Different Now": Chuang Tzu, cf. RP174fn, BW54fn.

"Reading Olav Hauge in the Dead of Winter": *The Bullfinch Rising from the Cherry Tree: Poems,* by Olav H. Hauge, trans. Robert Hedin, Brooding Heron Press, 2001, unpaginated.

"The Woodcutter": RP21fn, BW1.

"What Would I Do Without Her? or, The Hypocrite Tells the Truth for Once": RP182.

PART FOUR

"Well, Most of the Time Anyway": RP195.

"What Is Going On Here?": first quote, BW44, RP106; second quote, Chuang Tzu, *Chuang Tzu: The Inner Chapters,* trans. David Hinton, Counterpoint, 1997, p. 42.

"Dialogue": RP81&145&149, BW30&64.

"The Mountain Recluse Asks Himself a Question": RP86.

"The Beautiful People": RP57.

"Again Just Now": RP51.

"He Grieves": RP36.

"The World Left Behind": RP34, BW41.

"Ugly Americans": quotation cited in Lewis Hanke's *Aristotle and the American Indians* and cited in an unpublished monograph by Donald A. Gall entitled *Marginal Religion Among the Lakota Sioux: A Study of Conflict in Values and the Indian Mission of the United Church of Christ.*

"The Rich Are Never Satisfied": RP41.

"Sympathy for the Poor": RP60.

"April 3, 2003": quotation from *The New York Times*, April 3, 2003.

"Written While Riding the Q Train across Manhattan Bridge into Chinatown in a City I Once Called Home; or, Self-Pity in the City": RP17.

"Look at Her Now": RP20, BW9.

"Now Look at Me": quotation from *The Zen Poems of Ryōkan*, trans. Nobuyuki Yuasa, Princeton University Press, 1981, p. 65.

"Judevine Mountain's Siren Song: Upon Returning Home from the City": RP28, BW5.

PART FIVE

"What It Takes": RP31, BW2.

"Summer's Here": *I Don't Bow to Buddhas: Selected Poems of Yuan Mei*, trans. J.P. Seaton, Copper Canyon Press, 1997, p. 78.

"After a Painting by Tu Chin Called *The Scholar Fu Sheng in a Garden*": painting by Tu Chin (1465–1509), Metropolitan Museum of Art, New York.

"With Hui-neng": RP30fn, BW67; *100 Selected Poems by e. e. cummings*, Grove Press, 1959, p. 23.

"The Old Tree": RP198, BW65.

"The Way Is like Language": RP177.

"No Escape": RP26, GS7.

"Where I Went to School": RP102, AT17.

"The Evolution of Soph": RP117.

"When Han Shan Was Twenty-nine": RP34.

"Questions": RP131, BW38.

"Ryōkan Says": *The Zen Poems of Ryōkan*, trans. Nobuyuki Yuasa, Princeton Univesity Press, 1981, p. 62.

"Walking Meditation": *When I Find You Again, It Will Be in Mountains: Selected Poems of Chia Tao*, trans. Mike O'Connor, Wisdom Publications, 2000, p. 93.

"Glad to Be Who They Are": RP109; my own translation of chapter 81 of Lao Tzu's *Tao Te Ching* that is based mostly on the Gia-fu Feng/Jane English translation, Vintage Books, 1989, p. 82.

"My Father": RP21, BW1.

"Like Smoke from Our Campfire": RP86.

"Too Busy": RP165, BW88, AT23.

"The Busy Man Speaks": RP180, GS19.

"Poem with a Quotation from Mr. Lin": quotation from *The Chinese Art of Tea,* by John Blofeld, Shambhala, 1997, p. 49.

"The End of August": epigraph from "After Apple-Picking," *Complete Poems of Robert Frost,* Holt, Rinehart and Winston, 1949, p. 88.

PART SIX

"A Nameless Ghost": AT13, RP25&69.

"All Ye Who Are Doubtful and Confused": Jesus, Matthew 18:3, Revised Standard Version; Lao Tzu, my own translations, various and throughout, *Tao Te Ching;* John Coltrane, as quoted by Art Blakey, *Coda: The Jazz Magazine,* issue 173, June 1, 1980; Chuang Tzu, *Chuang Tzu: The Inner Chapters,* trans. David Hinton, Counterpoint, 1997, p. 25.

"Carnal Vision": RP141.

"A Question": RP185.

"That Rebellious Streak Always Did Him In": RP119.

"A Cave on Judevine Mountain": RP163, BW89, AT22.

"Learning Patience": Psalm 27:14, King James Version.

"The Woodcutter Changes His Mind": RP158, BW93.

"What Good Is This?": RP70, BW71.

"It's Now or Never": RP56, BW12.

"Unnamed in the Records of Immortals": RP18, BW29, GS4.

"My House": RP181.

"Making a Poem by Quoting Issa": various and throughout, *The Spring of My Life and Selected Haiku,* by Kobayashi Issa, trans. Sam Hamill, Shambhala, 1997.

PART SEVEN

"What Have I Got to Complain About?": RP172, BW16.

"South China Tiger, Green Mountain Catamount": RP147fn.

"Tomorrow": RP145.

About the Author

David Budbill was born in Cleveland, Ohio, in 1940 to a streetcar driver and a minister's daughter.

He is the author of *Judevine: The Complete Poems,* on which the play *Judevine* is based. *Judevine: The Play* has now been produced more than 50 times in 23 states. San Francisco's American Conservatory Theatre's production of *Judevine* won the Bay Area Critics' Circle Award for Best Ensemble Performance in 1991.

Budbill's latest CD, with bassist William Parker and drummer Hamid Drake, is *Songs for a Suffering World: A Prayer for Peace, a Protest Against War* (Boxholder Records, 2003). David's two-CD set *Zen Mountains— Zen Streets: A Duet for Poet and Improvised Bass,* with William Parker, was released in 1999, also on the Boxholder Records label.

David wrote the libretto for Erik Nielsen's *A Fleeting Animal: An Opera from Judevine,* which premiered in 2000.

Budbill edits and publishes *The Judevine Mountain Emailite: An On-line and On-going Journal of Politics and Opinion,* available on his Web site at http://www.davidbudbill.com.

He lives in the mountains of northern Vermont with his wife, the painter Lois Eby.

The Chinese character for poetry is made up of two parts: "word" and "temple." It also serves as pressmark for Copper Canyon Press. Founded in 1972, Copper Canyon Press remains dedicated to publishing poetry exclusively, from Nobel laureates to new and emerging authors. The Press thrives with the generous patronage of readers, writers, booksellers, librarians, teachers, students, and funders — everyone who shares the conviction that poetry invigorates the language and sharpens our appreciation of the world.

Major funding has been provided by:

The Paul G. Allen Family Foundation

Lannan Foundation

National Endowment for the Arts

The Starbucks Foundation

Washington State Arts Commission

For information and catalogs:

COPPER CANYON PRESS
Post Office Box 271
Port Townsend, Washington 98368
360-385-4925
www.coppercanyonpress.org

This book is set in Minion, designed for digital composition by Robert Slimbach in 1989. Minion is a contemporary typeface retaining elements of the pen-drawn letterforms developed during the Renaissance. Obelisk, by Phill Grimshaw, is used for the book and section titles. Book design by Valerie Brewster, Scribe Typography. Printed on archival-quality Glatfelter Author's Text at MacNaughton & Gunn, Inc.

← barcode